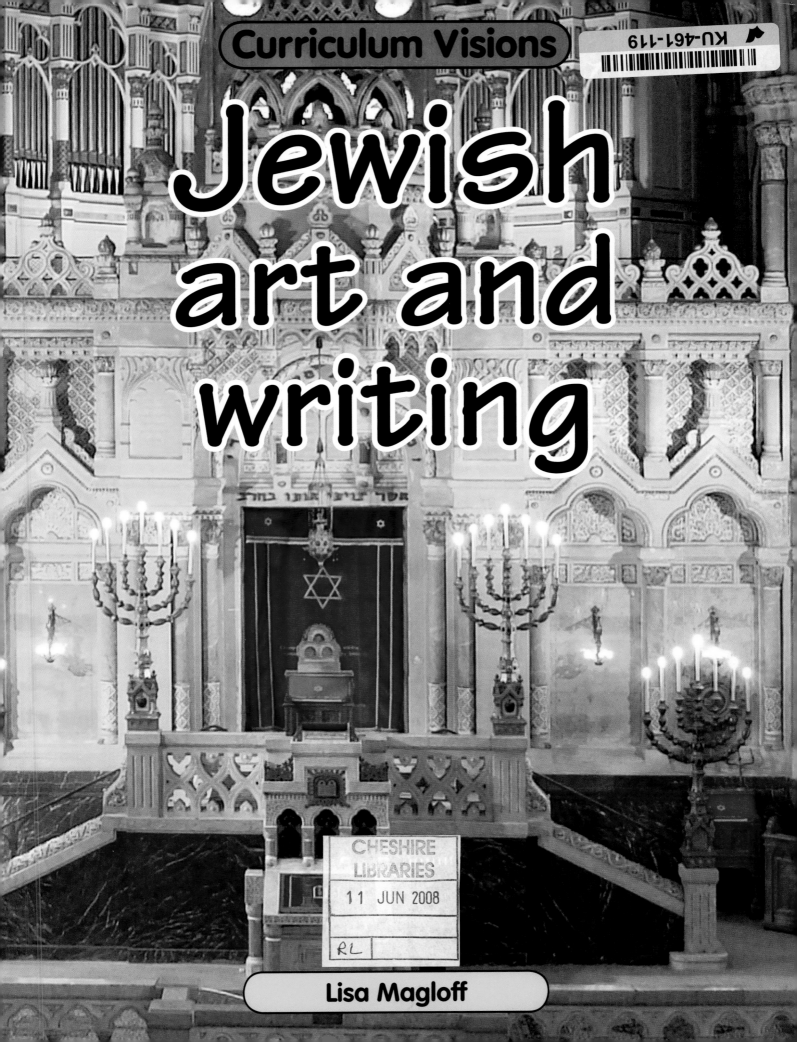

Curriculum Visions

Jewish art and writing

Lisa Magloff

Glossary

ARK This is the cabinet in which the Torah scrolls are kept in the synagogue. The word Ark is a shorter way of saying the Hebrew name of the cabinet: Aron Kodesh.

HEBREW The language spoken by the ancient Jews and the language of modern Israel. Jewish people are sometimes referred to as Hebrews or Hebrew people.

ISRAELITE/ISRAELI The descendents of Abraham were called Israelites (from the name Israel, the name God gave to Abraham's grandson Jacob).

JEW A person who follows the Jewish faith, or any person whose mother was a Jew or converted to Judaism. The word 'Jew' (in Hebrew, 'Yehudi') comes from the name Judah, which was the name of one of Jacob's twelve sons (Jacob was the son of Abraham, who the Bible says made an agreement with God to follow only God and no one else). Originally, the term Jew referred only to members of the tribe of Judah. However, the nation of Israel was once split into two kingdoms – Judah and Israel – and in ancient times, the people of Israel were taken into captivity in Babylon. The people of Judea were left behind, so after this time, all the Israelites were referred to as Jews.

JUDAH see **JEW**, above.

JUDAISM The religion of the Jewish people.

KIPPAH Also called a skullcap, this is a small cap that is worn by most Jewish men during worship in the synagogue. Some men wear the kippah all the time.

MATZAH A bread that is unleavened – it has no yeast in it so it is flat and does not rise. It is served during the holiday of Passover as a reminder of a time when the Jews left Egypt in such a hurry that their bread dough did not have time to rise.

MENORAH A candelabrum. It usually refers to a seven or nine-branched candelabrum in the synagogue, or an eight-branched candelabrum used during Chanukkah.

MEZUZAH A small box which contains a tiny scroll with some phrases from the Jewish Bible. Jews place a mezuzah on doorposts in their home because a commandment in the Jewish Bible tells the Jews to place the phrases on their doorposts.

MITZVAH The Hebrew word for commandment, or good deed.

PASSOVER Also called Pesach, this holiday remembers the time when the Jews were slaves in Egypt, and God sent ten plagues on the Egyptians. One of the plagues was the killing of the Egyptian first-born, but the Jewish first-born were 'passed over' and not killed.

SHABBAT The Hebrew word for Sabbath. The Jewish Sabbath lasts from sundown Friday to sundown Saturday.

SHOFAR A ram's horn, blown like a trumpet as a call to repentance on Rosh Hashanah.

SYMBOL An object, image, picture or letter that has a special meaning. Some symbols can have more than one meaning.

SYNAGOGUE The Jewish house of worship.

TALLIT The Jewish prayer shawl. This is worn by some adult men and women when they pray in the synagogue. The tallit is worn because of a Jewish commandment from God that they should always wear fringes on the corners of their clothing. The tallit has fringes on the ends, so Jews wear it to obey the commandment.

TEMPLE This is another word for synagogue. The original Temple was the central place of worship in ancient Jerusalem, where prayers and animal sacrifices were offered to God. The Temple was destroyed twice in ancient times, the last time by the Romans in 70 CE. After this it was never rebuilt. The Western Wall of the Temple, in Jerusalem, is the only part of the ancient building that can still be seen and is considered a holy site for Jews.

TORAH The Jewish Bible. The word Torah refers to both the first five books of the Bible, sometimes called the Books of Moses, or the Pentateuch, and to the entire body of Jewish teachings. In synagogues, the Torah is written on long scrolls and kept in a special case.

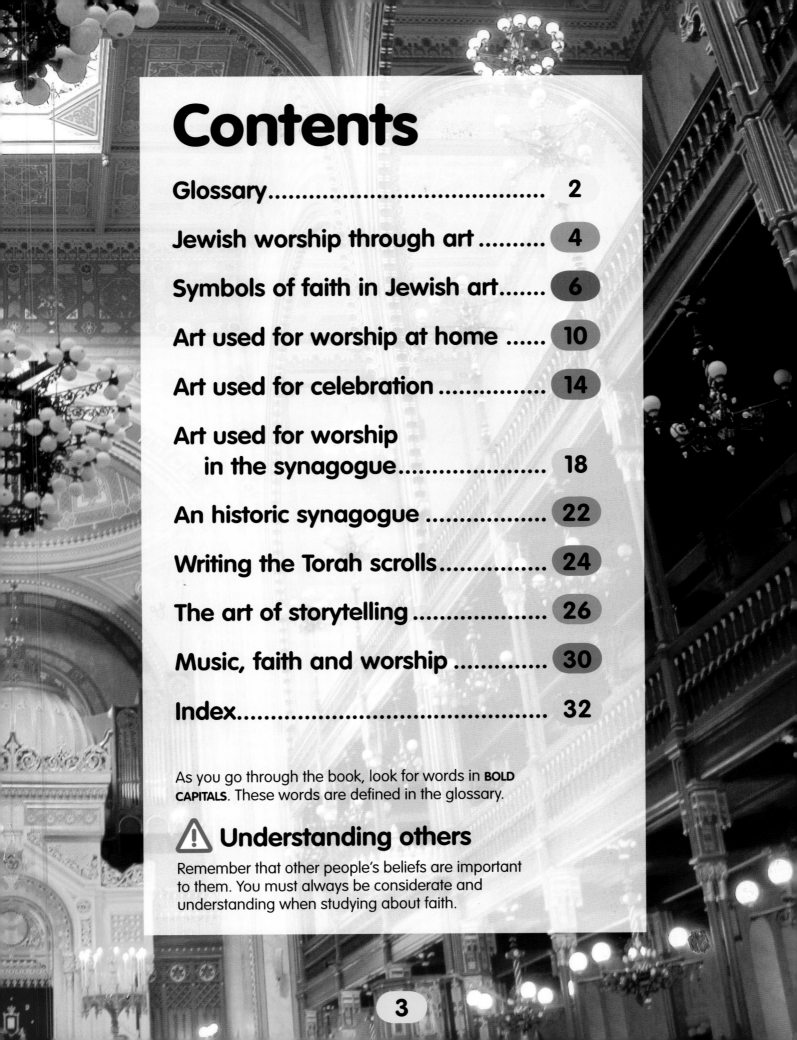

Contents

As you go through the book, look for words in **BOLD CAPITALS**. These words are defined in the glossary.

⚠️ Understanding others

Remember that other people's beliefs are important to them. You must always be considerate and understanding when studying about faith.

Jewish worship through art

Jews use many different types of art to show their faith.

▼ Decorative cup with menorah design.

People show their faith in many ways. For example, through prayer. But there are many other ways that people can express their faith.

Art is anything that people create in order to express ideas, thoughts or feelings. Many people show their faith through arts, such as painting, sculpture, writing or music. These arts can remind us of important things and teach us stories and ideas. Many religions also use symbols to help teach important ideas. All of these ways of expression can be just as meaningful as prayer.

Jewish people use many types of art to show their faith. Much Jewish art helps to remind worshippers of the long history of Judaism around the world.

Other Jewish art helps people to worship. For example, the Jewish holy book is written in a special script and often 'sung' out loud during worship.

Art also plays a role in everyday life for many Jewish people. Items used in daily or weekly worship at home, such as candlesticks, are made to remind people that God created

beauty. On holidays, special foods are cooked and eaten that help remind people of important events.

Some Jewish people also wear special items of clothing every day in order to remind them of God's commandments and God's presence.

Images, such as stained glass, are mainly used in synagogues.

The design of the synagogue, and of all the things that are inside it, are also used as reminders of Jewish history and ideals.

As you read through this book, you will have a chance to explore many of the different ways in which Jewish people use art in the practice of their faith.

▲ Worshippers with Torah scrolls. The cloth that covers the scrolls has the first words of the 10 commandments written in Hebrew.

Symbols of faith in Jewish art

Designs and patterns may look simple, but they can have many different meanings.

Judaism began in the Middle East. As Jewish people spread around the world to places far from the Middle East, they began to use different symbols as a way to remind themselves and others of their Jewish identity and history.

For example, one of the most common symbols of Judaism, the Star of David, or Shield of David (called the Magen David in Hebrew) did not begin to be used as a symbol of Judaism until the 16th or 17th century. Other symbols began to be used at different times. Here are a few of them.

The Star of David

The shape of the Star of David is said to be a reminder of the shape of the shield of the ancient Jewish king who founded Jerusalem – King David. This type of shape was also a common good luck symbol in ancient times.

The shape of the star has many meanings. The top triangle points upwards, towards God, while the lower triangle points downwards, towards the world. This may be a reminder that it is important to both worship God and to help make the world a better place. The triangles are connected together and cannot be separated. This is a reminder that the Jewish people, wherever they live, are also connected by their beliefs.

Beginning in the 17th century, it became a popular practice to put this symbol on the outside of synagogues, to identify them as Jewish houses of worship, in the same way that a cross identified a Christian house of worship.

Later, when the modern country of Israel was founded, the Star of David was used as a national symbol and put on the flag.

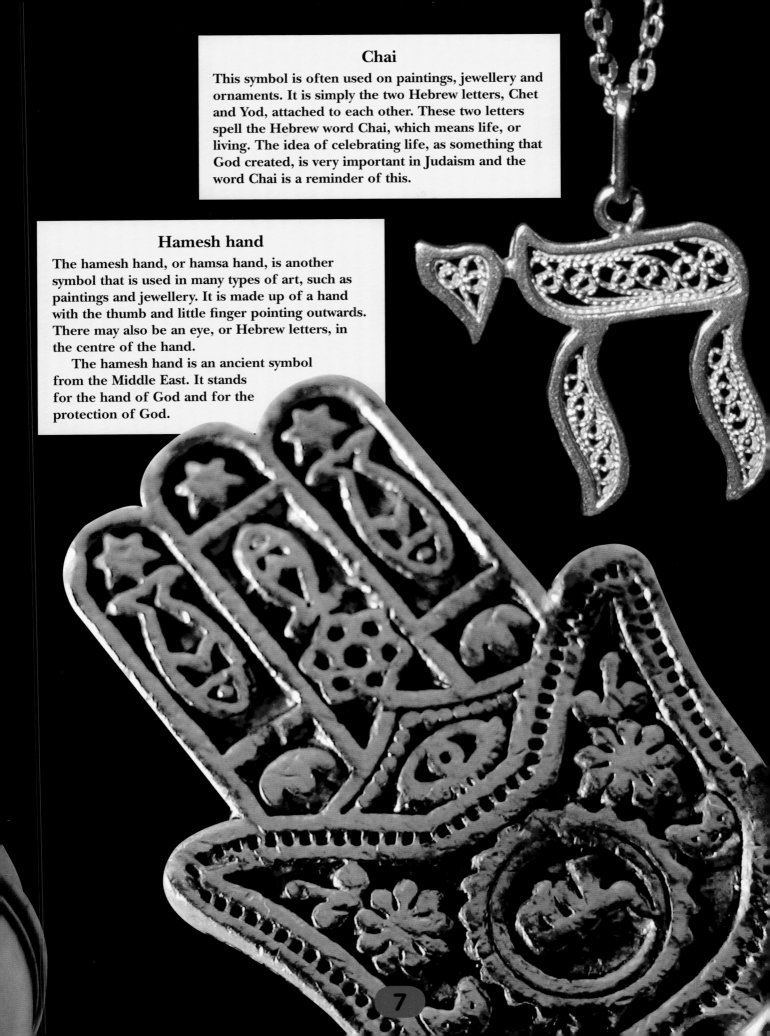

Chai

This symbol is often used on paintings, jewellery and ornaments. It is simply the two Hebrew letters, Chet and Yod, attached to each other. These two letters spell the Hebrew word Chai, which means life, or living. The idea of celebrating life, as something that God created, is very important in Judaism and the word Chai is a reminder of this.

Hamesh hand

The hamesh hand, or hamsa hand, is another symbol that is used in many types of art, such as paintings and jewellery. It is made up of a hand with the thumb and little finger pointing outwards. There may also be an eye, or Hebrew letters, in the centre of the hand.

The hamesh hand is an ancient symbol from the Middle East. It stands for the hand of God and for the protection of God.

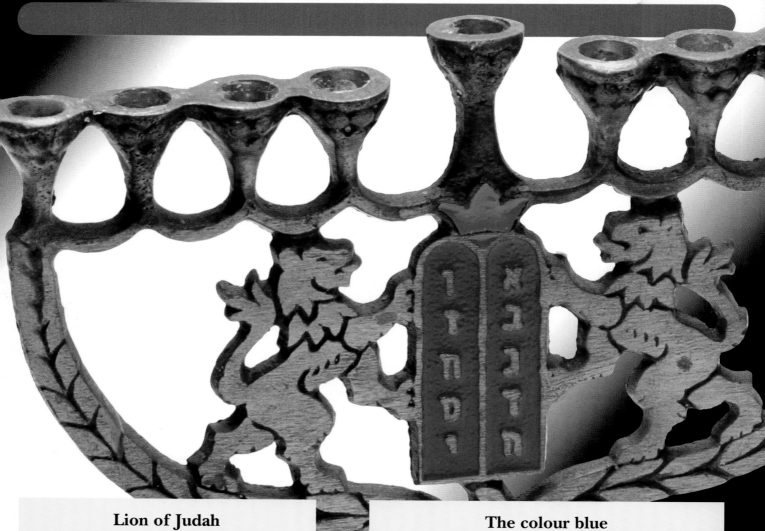

Lion of Judah

Judah was the name of the leader of an ancient group of Jews, and the lion has been an important Jewish symbol since ancient times. The Jewish Bible, the Torah, mentions lions 150 times. The lion stands for strength and the ability to protect and to save others.

In ancient Jewish art, sculptures of lions are used to guard the Temple and the Holy Ark inside the Temple. Later, sculptures of lions were placed outside synagogues and were made into mosaics for the entrances to synagogues and homes. Lions are also used as decoration on the cloth that covers the Torah in the synagogue, and on paintings and drawings.

The colour blue

The colour blue has special meaning in Judaism and in Jewish art. If you look at the Israeli flag, you will notice that the only colours on it are blue and white. The Jewish prayer shawl, or tallit, which is worn in synagogues also has the colour blue on it.

In ancient times, a blue dye was made from a type of snail. This was a very expensive dye to make and so it was only used on the curtains that covered the Ark in the ancient Temple, for clothing for priests and nobles, and for wall hangings in royal palaces.

The colour blue is also mentioned as important many times in the Torah. For example, bonds of wisdom are compared to 'a cord of blue', and Moses is said to wear blue clothing.

In ancient times, blue dye was also used to colour the threads on the four corners of the tallit. This was to fulfil a commandment in the Jewish Bible: "The Lord said to Moses as follows: Speak to the Israelite people and instruct them to make for themselves fringes on the corners of their garments throughout the ages; let them attach a cord of blue to the fringe at each corner." Today, the fringes on the prayer shawl still have blue thread in them.

The crown

Beginning in around the 16th century, the crown symbol began to be used in Jewish art. Metal crowns may be used to decorate the Torah scroll, or crowns may be embroidered onto the cloth that covers the scroll, or the curtains that cover the Ark in the synagogue. Sometimes, a crown is shown carried by lions.

The crown stands for royalty, and it helps to show the importance of the Jewish Bible (the Torah). Because Jews believe that God wrote the Torah, placing a crown on the Jewish Bible is also a reminder that God is king.

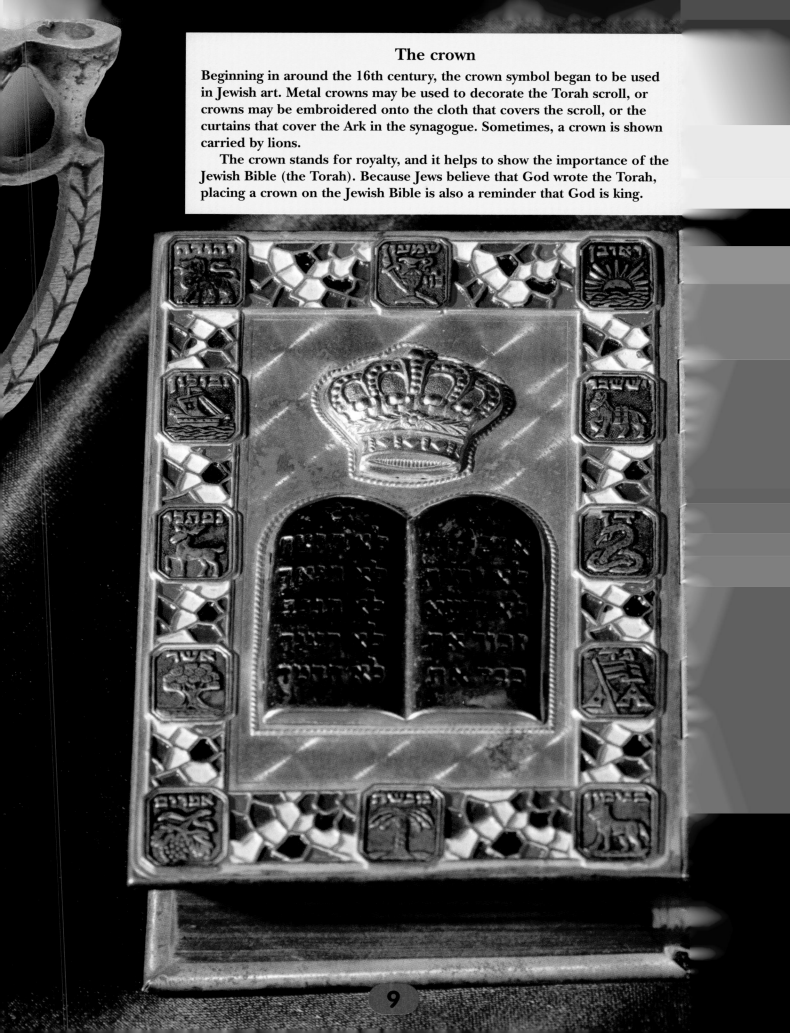

Art used for worship at home

Many types of Jewish art are actually used for worship at home.

The Jewish religion teaches the idea that the things used in worship should be beautiful as well as useful. In Hebrew, this idea is sometimes called hiddur mitzvah, which means 'making the commandments beautiful'. You can see this by looking at the many different ways that Jewish head coverings, called kippah, worn in synagogue are decorated. Because the kippah are worn during worship, many people want them to look as beautiful as possible.

Making high quality objects for worship is a way of showing love for God, whether in the synagogue or at home.

Mezuzah cases

On the door frames of many Jewish homes, you will find a small case. This case is called a mezuzah. The word mezuzah means doorpost, and the mezuzah is placed on the doorposts of the house.

Inside the mezuzah is a tiny scroll with passages from the Torah written on it.

Mezuzah can be made of any material, such as metal, ceramic, glass, wood or even plastic. They have the Hebrew letter shin on the outside. This is the first letter of the Hebrew word Shaddai, which is one of the names of God and means, 'Guardian of the doorways of Israel'.

Many mezuzah are also decorated with designs and are works of art. So, the mezuzah is a reminder of God's words, but it also helps to make the house look beautiful.

▲ A selection of different kippot (the word for more than one kippah is kippot).

▼ These ceramic mezuzah all have different designs on them. Note that they all have the Hebrew letter shin on the outside.

Weblink: www.CurriculumVisions.com

Art used for Shabbat

One of the ways that Jewish families show their faith is by having a meal together every Shabbat (the Jewish Sabbath, which lasts from sundown Friday to sundown Saturday). During the meal, prayers are said, candles are lit, wine is drunk, and a special type of bread may be eaten.

Many of the things used during the Shabbat meal, such as candle holders, a plate for the bread and a glass for the wine, have important meanings and so they are made to look attractive. They are a type of useful art.

If you look at the pictures on these pages, you can see some of the things used on Shabbat.

During the meal, the table is usually decorated with nice linen and china. This is a way of showing that the Shabbat day is more special than other days of the week.

At the beginning of Shabbat, just before sunset, blessings are said while two candles are lit. This is a reminder of the light of God, and a way to bring God's light into the house. The two candles are a reminder of the two commandments – to remember the Shabbat and to observe the Shabbat. The candles are usually in decorated holders which may be painted with designs.

A wine goblet, called a kiddush cup, is another work of art used on Shabbat. Kiddush is the name of the blessing which is recited over the wine before the meal begins. At the beginning of the Shabbat meal the cup is filled with wine. After the kiddush prayer has been said, everyone shares the wine.

The kiddush cup is sometimes made of a precious metal, such as silver, and is beautifully decorated. Many cups are passed down from generation to generation as family heirlooms.

לכבוד שבת ויום טוב

Next, a blessing is said over two loaves of braided egg bread, called hallah. There are two loaves because they are a reminder of the time after the Jews escaped from slavery in Egypt and lived in the wilderness; God sent a food called manna from heaven to feed everyone, and on Friday God sent twice as much manna as on other days.

Adding eggs to the bread made it taste richer. This is a reminder that Shabbat is different from the other days of the week, when bread is made only with flour and water. Hallah is usually made with six strands – this is a reminder of the six days of the week.

A cloth 'hallah cover' is used to cover the two loaves of bread. Many hallah covers are decorated with Hebrew words or pictures of objects found on the Shabbat table.

At the end of Shabbat, on Saturday evening, there is another ceremony called Havdalah, or separation. During this ceremony blessings are recited over wine, candles and spices, which are kept in a decorated spice box that is passed around for everyone to smell. The sweet smell of the spices stands for the hope that the sweetness of Shabbat will be remembered all week long. The spice box is often made from wood or precious metal and is usually decorated with designs.

A special blue and white braided candle with two wicks is used during the havdalah blessings. The light stands for the hope that the new week will be full of brightness and joy. The candle has two wicks because the commandment is to say a blessing over "illuminations of fire" – illuminations is plural, so two wicks, or two candles are used.

Art used for celebration

Many types of practical arts are used to help people celebrate holidays and special occasions.

Many kinds of art are used to help people celebrate holidays throughout the Jewish year. These arts include painted or decorated ceramic dishes and plates, cast metal or ceramic candle holders, carved and decorated boxes and embroidered or painted clothing.

Having specially decorated plates, cups, candle holders and other practical items helps to remind people that holidays are an important time and are different from other days.

Here are a few of the ways that art is used to help celebrate holidays or other special days in a practical way.

▲▼ A Chanukkah menorah with all of the candles lit, and a dreidel.

Ketubah

A ketubah is a wedding contract. On the ketubah, the bride and groom have written the things that they promise to do for each other in their married life, such as to love each other and care for each other. The ketubah is usually written in calligraphy and decorated with designs. Many people frame their ketubah and hang it on the wall of their homes.

On the holiday of Chanukkah, candles are lit in an eight-branched candle holder called a menorah. The menorah also has a ninth candle, which is called the helper candle and is used to light the other eight. There is no special design for the menorah, but most of them are made to look beautiful. Each night one more candle is lit.

Chanukkah remembers a miracle when a single day's amount of sacred oil lasted for eight days, so another way to celebrate the holiday is to eat fried foods, like doughnuts and fried potato pancakes.

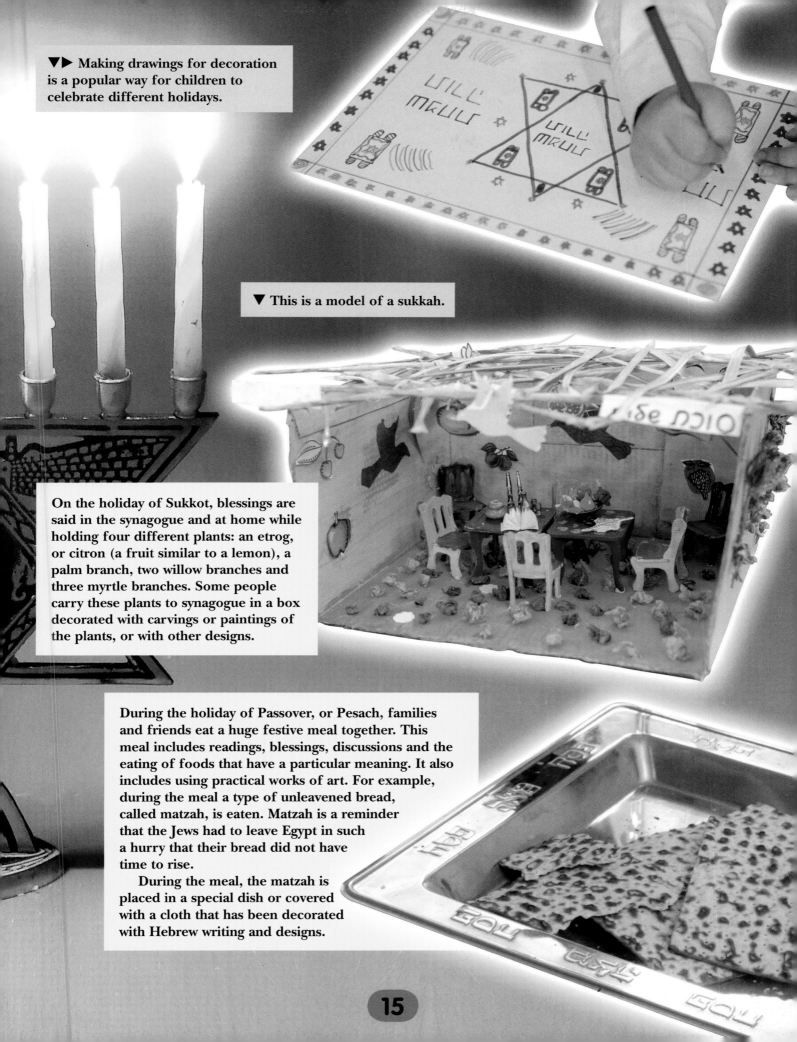

▼▶ Making drawings for decoration is a popular way for children to celebrate different holidays.

▼ This is a model of a sukkah.

On the holiday of Sukkot, blessings are said in the synagogue and at home while holding four different plants: an etrog, or citron (a fruit similar to a lemon), a palm branch, two willow branches and three myrtle branches. Some people carry these plants to synagogue in a box decorated with carvings or paintings of the plants, or with other designs.

During the holiday of Passover, or Pesach, families and friends eat a huge festive meal together. This meal includes readings, blessings, discussions and the eating of foods that have a particular meaning. It also includes using practical works of art. For example, during the meal a type of unleavened bread, called matzah, is eaten. Matzah is a reminder that the Jews had to leave Egypt in such a hurry that their bread did not have time to rise.

During the meal, the matzah is placed in a special dish or covered with a cloth that has been decorated with Hebrew writing and designs.

The New Year's holiday, Rosh Hashanah, is often celebrated by eating slices of apple dipped in honey, as a reminder of the hopes for a sweet new year. The honey may be served in a glass or ceramic honey dish in the shape of an apple, or decorated with apple designs.

Particular foods are eaten throughout the Pesach meal. Each of these foods also has a special meaning. These foods are usually all kept on a large plate that has been decorated with the name of each food, and often, with paintings of the foods.

מרזר

ביצה

זרזע

פסח

כרפס

חרזסת

חזרת

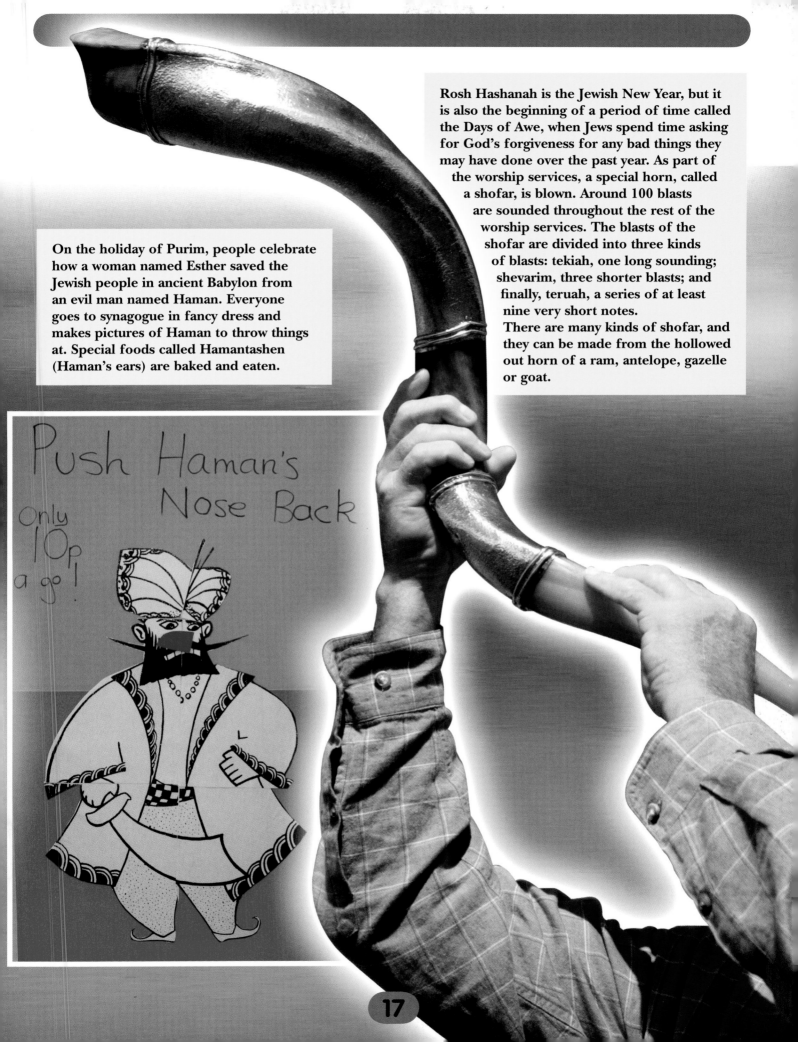

On the holiday of Purim, people celebrate how a woman named Esther saved the Jewish people in ancient Babylon from an evil man named Haman. Everyone goes to synagogue in fancy dress and makes pictures of Haman to throw things at. Special foods called Hamantashen (Haman's ears) are baked and eaten.

Rosh Hashanah is the Jewish New Year, but it is also the beginning of a period of time called the Days of Awe, when Jews spend time asking for God's forgiveness for any bad things they may have done over the past year. As part of the worship services, a special horn, called a shofar, is blown. Around 100 blasts are sounded throughout the rest of the worship services. The blasts of the shofar are divided into three kinds of blasts: tekiah, one long sounding; shevarim, three shorter blasts; and finally, teruah, a series of at least nine very short notes.

There are many kinds of shofar, and they can be made from the hollowed out horn of a ram, antelope, gazelle or goat.

Art used for worship in the synagogue

Since the destruction of the Temple in Jerusalem, when the ancient Romans forced all the Jews to leave Jerusalem, Jews spread out to live in almost all the countries of the world. So, over time, Jewish artists began to make many types of art and objects to remind people of their Jewish identity and culture.

Windows

In many synagogues, plain or stained glass windows are used to remind people of their heritage. For example, synagogue windows are often curved at the top and square at the bottom, as a reminder of the shape of the tablets containing the 10 commandments that God gave to Moses on Mount Sinai.

In some synagogues, there may be twelve windows around the main prayer hall, as a reminder of the Twelve Tribes of Israel mentioned in the Jewish Bible. In other synagogues, there are stained glass windows with scenes from the stories in the Torah.

The windows may also be a reminder of the part of the Torah where God creates light, and also of the part of the Torah where God tells the Jewish people to "be a light unto nations".

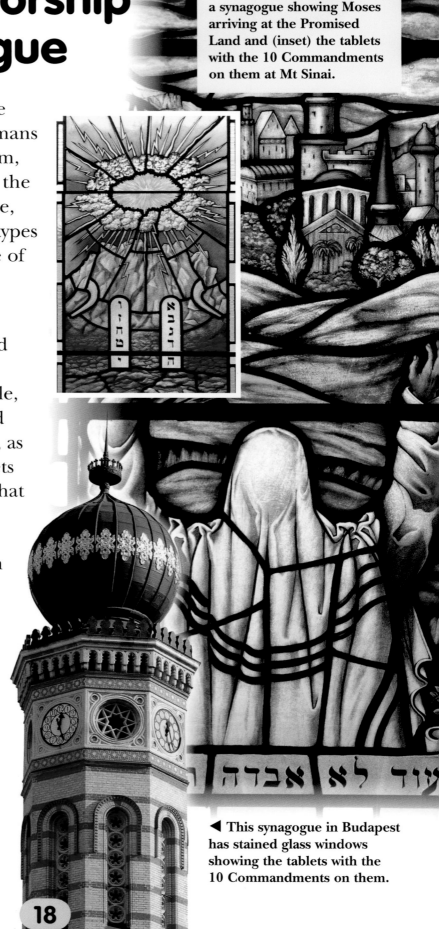

▼ Stained glass windows in a synagogue showing Moses arriving at the Promised Land and (inset) the tablets with the 10 Commandments on them at Mt Sinai.

◀ This synagogue in Budapest has stained glass windows showing the tablets with the 10 Commandments on them.

Dressing the Torah scrolls

Some art is used to remind worshippers of the ancient Temple in Jerusalem. For example, the Torah scrolls that are used in the synagogue are covered in cloth and ornaments. These are reminders of the clothing worn by the High Priest of the Temple in Jerusalem. This clothing included a tunic (the Torah mantle, or covering), a belt (the sash around the Torah scroll), a tall hat (the crown of the Torah), and a breastplate.

There are also other scrolls used for worship in the synagogue. The most important of these is the Megillah, or Book of Esther. This is read out loud during the festival of Purim. These scrolls are kept in a separate case, which may be made out of metal, cloth or wood and decorated with designs.

Crown

Breastplate

The crown is usually decorated with small bells, like the bells that were once sewn onto the robe of the High Priest so that people could hear the High Priest as he moved during worship.

Yad

The breastplate is encrusted with 12 precious or semi-precious stones that stand for the 12 Tribes of Israel.

The menorah.

The Ark.

The Ark and menorah

The cabinet, or Ark, that holds the Torah scrolls in the synagogue is a reminder of the cabinet used in the ancient Temple. It may be made out of wood, marble or another material and decorated with designs or carvings that remind people of the Torah.

The menorah used in the synagogue is another reminder of the Temple.

The story of the first menorah is told in the Torah. After the Jewish people escaped from slavery in Egypt, they spent 40 years wandering in the desert. During that time, they built a temporary place for worship, called the tabernacle, which they carried around with them. The Torah (Exodus 25:31–40) describes how God asked the artist Bezalel to build a huge golden candle holder to place next to the tabernacle during worship.

Once the Jewish people settled in Israel and built the Temple, the menorah was placed in the Temple.

So, today, the menorah in the synagogue is a reminder of the time the Jews escaped from slavery in Egypt and of how God helped them to survive in the desert. The six branches are a reminder that God created the world in six days.

▲ Ner tamid.

The middle part stands for the seventh day, the day of rest. So the menorah is also a reminder of the story about how the world was created and why the seventh day is a day of rest.

Yad

Because the Torah scrolls are very valuable, they are not supposed to be touched. This is because the oils from your hands can harm the scrolls. So when they are read a special pointer, called a yad, is used. Yad means hand and the yad is usually shaped like a hand and is made from metal or carved from wood.

The ner tamid

The ner tamid is also called the eternal light. It is usually hung up in front of the Ark. It stands for the commandment to always keep a light burning outside of the Ark. It may be made of brass or another metal, and hung on chains.

◀▶ Yads.

An historic synagogue

Even though all synagogues look different, you can learn a lot about Jewish ideals by examining the architecture of an historic synagogue.

There are no rules for how a synagogue should look, so every synagogue is different. Many synagogues are designed to show the ideals of the Jewish community and its history. You can see this by looking at the design of the historic Bevis Marks synagogue in London, the oldest synagogue in Britain which is still in use.

You can see that even though this synagogue was built in England, some parts of it are designed to look like a Spanish or Portuguese synagogue. This is because the Bevis Marks synagogue was built in 1701 by Jews who had come to England from Amsterdam, and their families had, in turn, originally come from Spain and Portugal.

In Spain and Portugal, the tradition is that the seats are arranged around the outside of the main prayer room, or sanctuary, facing the centre, and this explains the arrangement of the seats in the Bevis Marks synagogue.

Other parts of the synagogue, such as the menorah, the Ark and the Star of David, are similar to those found in almost all synagogues.

In the centre of the prayer hall are seven hanging candelabra that are still used to light the building with candlelight on holy days. The seven candelabra stand for the seven days of the week.

The meal that money can't buy

A Roman Emperor once visited the house of a very poor Jewish family. To his surprise he found them laughing and singing, as if they were at a feast – even though there was very little food on the table and it looked like very simple food.

When the family saw the Emperor outside, they invited him in to join them and soon he was eating some of the most delicious food he had ever tasted.

When he returned to the palace, the Emperor summoned his cooks and described what he had eaten. He ordered them to prepare a similar meal, but try as they might, it never tasted the same as the food he had eaten in that poverty stricken house.

Eventually, in desperation, he sent for the head of the Jewish family and asked him what was in the food that he had missed out.

"The Sabbath food contains an ingredient that, with all your wealth, you cannot buy," replied the man. "It is the finest spice there is. When it is added to food it changes even a snack into a banquet."

When he heard this, the Emperor knew he had to have that spice. "Tell me what it is and I shall buy it, no matter what the cost," ordered the Emperor.

"I'm afraid you can't buy it at any price," answered the man. "It's called Shabbat."

Hershel and the stone soup

Hershel Ostropolier had to live by his wits. Sometimes he made a good living; sometimes he didn't. One thing Hershel loved was to eat delicious meals, but these were few and far between.

One day Hershel came to the town of Vishnitz. When the townspeople saw him coming they began to shout "Here comes Hershel! Here comes Hershel! We have little enough for ourselves. We don't need a big mouth like that." They hurried to hide their food.

Hershel stopped first at the house of Shaiah the miller. "Could you spare a bit of food for an old friend who is so hungry?"

"Hershel, I've had no food for myself and my family for three days," Shaiah said sadly. "A drought has made for a poor harvest."

Everywhere Hershel went it was the same. Velvel the innkeeper said that all the food had been eaten by his lodgers and every bed was taken. Avrum the butcher said he was out of meat.

Hershel, being really hungry, knew he had to think quickly. He called out to the townspeople. "Friends, come near. I am a hungry man. I have asked you for food but you have no food. Well then, we'll have to make stone soup."

The townspeople stared at Hershel. Some thought he was crazy, but they also thought that maybe, just maybe, this was a new recipe that everyone would want to learn to make.

"First we'll need a large iron pot," Hershel yelled. A huge pot was filled with water, a fire was started and the pot was set to boil.

"And now, if you please," said Hershel, "three round, smooth stones." The stones were brought and Hershel plopped them into the water.

"Any soup needs salt and pepper," said Hershel, as he began to stir. Children ran to fetch salt and pepper.

"Stones like these generally make good soup. But oh, if there were cabbages and potatoes and carrots and onions, it would be much better." Velvel thought he could contribute a little of these vegetables and sent his children off to the pantry to fetch some.

Hershel cut up the vegetables. "If only we had a bit of meat, this soup would be good enough for a rich man's table. But no use asking for what you don't have."

"I think I could find some scraps of meat somewhere," said Avrum. He hurried to his shop and came back with a few pounds of meat and some marrow bones.

Other townspeople went back to their homes and returned with more vegetables and beef to put into the pot of stone soup.

"Ah," sighed Hershel, as he stirred the hearty broth. "If only we had a little barley, this soup would be fit for the czar himself. But – no use asking for what you don't have," Hershel sighed.

Shaiah the miller sent a servant back to the mill to fetch a sack of barley.

At last the soup was ready. Long tables were placed in the town square. All around were lighted torches.

Such a soup! How good it smelled! But then the townspeople asked themselves, "Would not such a soup require bread and wine?" So they brought out bread and wine.

Never had there been such a feast in Vishnitz. Never had the townspeople tasted such soup. And fancy this! It was made from stones.

They ate and drank. After a while the musicians got a fiddle and a clarinet and an accordion and played a few tunes. The people danced and sang into the night.

At last they were tired. Then Hershel asked, "Velvel, is there not a room at your inn where I could sleep?"

"Anyone who can make such a feast out of nothing but stones deserves the best bed in the inn!" So Hershel slept on the most comfortable bed in Velvel's inn.

In the morning all the townspeople gathered in the square to wish Hershel well on his journey.

"Thank God for what you have taught us," the townspeople said to Hershel. "We shall never go hungry, now that we know how to make soup from stones."

"You are welcome," said Hershel. "It's all in knowing how." And off he went down the road to the next town.

Music, faith and worship

Music is used in the Jewish faith for many purposes.

Music used in worship

In ancient times, the priests in the Temple chanted the prayers from the Torah. After the Temple was destroyed, people continued to chant the prayers and readings.

During worship in the synagogue, parts of the Torah may be chanted, or 'sung', out loud. The chanting may be done by a choir, by the worshippers or by a person called a cantor (which means singer), or chazzan, who has been specially trained in the proper chants and songs to use during worship.

Singing helps to make the words more dramatic. Singing, or chanting, instead of reading also helps to make the words come alive and to sound more beautiful.

Music in celebration

Over time, many popular songs began to be used during Jewish holidays and celebrations. Some of these songs were written in Hebrew, and others were written in local languages. Many of these songs are often sung at home during holidays. Others are sung during community celebrations, such as weddings.

Other popular songs are sung as reminders of Jewish history. For example, many Yiddish songs were written by Jewish people who had left their homes in Eastern Europe and moved to America. Many of these songs remember their old homes and ways of life.

Hava Nagilah

This song is often sung at celebrations, such as weddings. The words are given in Hebrew and then in English.

Hava nagilah, Hava nagilah, Hava nagilah
    V'nismikha
Hava n'ranana, Hava n'ranana, Hava n'ranana
    V'nismikha
Uru, Uru akhim
Uru akhim b'lev s'mayakh
Uru akhim b'lev s'mayakh
Uru akhim b'lev s'mayakh
Uru akhim b'lev s'mayakh
Uru akhim
Uru akhim
B'lev somayakh

Come let's rejoice, Come let's rejoice,
    Come let's rejoice
And we'll be happy
Come let's celebrate, Come let's celebrate,
    Come let's celebrate
And we'll be happy
Arise, Arise brothers
Arise brothers with a happy heart
Arise brothers with a happy heart
Arise brothers with a happy heart
Arise brothers with a happy heart
Arise brothers
Arise brothers
With a happy heart

Beltz, Mayn Shtetele Beltz

This song was written in the mid-19th century, when many Jews were fleeing Russia and other places in Eastern Europe to escape mistreatment. The singer is remembering the home that he misses.

When I recall my childhood,
    I feel like I am having a dream.
How does the little house look,
    which used to sparkle with lights?
Does the little tree grow which I planted
    long ago?

Beltz, my little town!
The little house where I spent my childhood!
The poor little room where I used to laugh
    with other children!
Every Shabes I would run to the river bank
    to play with other children under a little
    green tree.
Beltz, my little town!
My little town where I had so many fine dreams!

The little house is old and overgrown with moss.
The old roof collapsed and the windows are
    without glass.
The attic is crooked, the walls bent.
I would never recognise it...

Index

Curriculum Visions

There's much more on-line including videos

You will find multimedia resources covering six different religions, as well as history, geography, science and spelling subjects in the subscription Professional Zone at:

www.CurriculumVisions.com

A CVP Book
Copyright Earthscape © 2008

The right of Lisa Magloff to be identified as the author of this work has been asserted by her in accordance with the Copyright, Designs and Patents Act 1988.

Author
Lisa Magloff, MA

Religious Adviser
Nathan Abrams, PhD

Senior Designer
Adele Humphries, BA

Editor
Gillian Gatehouse

Acknowledgements
The publishers would like to thank the following for their help and advice: Hendon Reform Synagogue, London; Bevis Marks Synagogue, London; Simon Marks school, London; the Bright family.

Photographs
The Earthscape Picture Library, except: (c=centre, t=top, b=bottom, l=left, r=right) *ShutterStock* pages 1, 2–3, 4–5, 6–7, 8–9, 10–11t, 12bl, 13tr, 14, 16b, 17r, 18b, 20, 21b, 25, 28–29, 31tr.

Designed and produced by
Earthscape

Printed in China by
WKT Company Ltd

Jewish art and writing
– Curriculum Visions
A CIP record for this book is available from the British Library
ISBN: 978 1 86214 249 7

This product is manufactured from sustainable managed forests. For every tree cut down at least one more is planted.